THE SHAPE OF A HUMAN

Abhijit Naskar is the twenty-first century Neuroscientist whose contributions in Cognitive and Behavioral Neuroscience have helped the world tackle the issues of mental illness, prejudice, hate, extremism, discrimination and segregation more effectively. As an untiring advocate of mental health and universal acceptance, he became a beloved best-selling author all over the world with his very first book "The Art of Neuroscience in Everything". With his pioneering ventures into the Neuropsychology of beliefs and biases, he has hugely contributed in the eradication of religious and cultural differences in our world, for which he is popularly hailed as the humanitarian scientist, who takes the human civilization in the path of sweet general harmony.

The Shape of A
HUMAN

Our America Their America

ABHIJIT NASKAR

The Shape of A Human:

Our America Their America

An Amazon Publishing Company, 1st Edition, 2021

Printed in the United States of America

ISBN: 9798707498633

Also by Abhijit Naskar

The Art of Neuroscience in Everything
Your Own Neuron: A Tour of Your Psychic Brain
The God Parasite: Revelation of Neuroscience
The Spirituality Engine
Love Sutra: The Neuroscientific Manual of Love
Homo: A Brief History of Consciousness
Neurosutra: The Abhijit Naskar Collection
Autobiography of God: Biopsy of A Cognitive Reality
Biopsy of Religions: Neuroanalysis towards Universal
Tolerance
Prescription: Treating India's Soul
What is Mind?
In Search of Divinity: Journey to The Kingdom of Conscience
Love, God & Neurons: Memoir of a scientist who found
himself by getting lost
The Islamophobic Civilization: Voyage of Acceptance
Neurons of Jesus: Mind of A Teacher, Spouse & Thinker
Neurons, Oxygen & Nanak
The Education Decree
Principia Humanitas
The Krishna Cancer
Rowdy Buddha: The First Sapiens
We Are All Black: A Treatise on Racism
The Bengal Tigress: A Treatise on Gender Equality
Either Civilized or Phobic: A Treatise on Homosexuality
Wise Mating: A Treatise on Monogamy
Illusion of Religion: A Treatise on Religious
Fundamentalism
The Film Testament
Human Making is Our Mission: A Treatise on Parenting
I Am The Thread: My Mission
7 Billion Gods: Humans Above All
Lord is My Sheep: Gospel of Human
Morality Absolute
A Push in Perception
Let The Poor Be Your God
Conscience over Nonsense
Saint of The Sapiens
Time to Save Medicine
Fabric of Humanity

Build Bridges not Walls: In the name of Americana
The Constitution of The United Peoples of Earth
Lives to Serve Before I Sleep
When Humans Unite: Making A World Without Borders
All For Acceptance
Monk Meets World
Mission Reality
Citizens of Peace: Beyond The Savagery of Sovereignty
Operation Justice: To Make A Society That Needs No Law
See No Gender
The Gospel of Technology
Every Generation Needs Caretakers: The Gospel of
Patriotism
Aşkanjali: The Sufi Sermon
Mad About Humans: World Maker's Almanac
Revolution Indomable
When Call The People: My World My Responsibility
No Foreigner Only Family
Hurricane Humans: Give me accountability, I'll give you
peace
Ain't Enough to Look Human
Servitude is Sanctitude
Time To End Democracy: The Meritocratic Manifesto
I Vicdansaadet Speaking: No Rest Till The World is Lifted
Boldly Comes Justice: Sentient not Silent
Good Scientist: When Science and Service Combine
Sleepless for Society
Neden Türk: The Gospel of Secularism
Martyr Meets World: To Solve The Hard Problem of
Inhumanity

DEDICATION

*This book is dedicated to my motherland -
my America, the land that adopted me as a son
when nobody knew I exist.*

CONTENTS

1.   Why America Exists

When oppression became unbearable, America was born - when discrimination turned extreme, America was born - when rigidity became intolerable, America was born. America was born of an unbending desire for freedom - America was born of a drive for self-correction - America was born of an urge for progression.

Yes we did many mistakes in the process, even committed horrible atrocities - we drove people off their lands to build a new world for our children - and nothing that we can do today can mend those atrocities of yesterday, but what we can do is to make a promise to ourselves to never repeat those atrocities of our ancestors no more.

It's time we become the new Americans - Americans with more accountability than recklessness - Americans with more curiosity than rigidity - Americans with more acceptability than prejudice - Americans with more inclusivity than discrimination.

There is no our America and their America, there's only one America - the United States of America. You see, ours is not just the United States of America, ours is the United States of

Assimilation. And we must practice this principle to the letter and spirit everyday of our lives.

For example, we of all people cannot in right mind deny shelter to those seeking refuge, especially when we are both sociologically and economically capable of doing so. Whoever comes to these shores of liberty, in the hope of life, freedom and happiness, automatically becomes an American, by measure of the same determination and will that made our founding fathers set foot on Plymouth Rock escaping British bigotry, snobbery and barbarism.

Our very country is founded by immigrants. America was built by refugees, and as such, if this land can't be a refuge for the subjugated and persecuted, then it is an insult on our very existence as the great land of the free and brave.

2. Backbone of America

Different civilizations in the world have different backbones. And the backbone of American civilization is liberty. Lady liberty is not just a statue, she is a reflection of the soul of America. Unlike most nations on earth, the soul of America is not rooted in religion, it's not rooted in ideology, it's not even rooted in nationality - the soul of America is rooted in a pure, uncorrupted, indomitable ambition for freedom.

No country is greater than another, for each country has its strongholds as well as shortfalls. And the stronghold of America is its exploratory spirit. What America explores today, the world explores a decade later. America is impossibility made possible. Nothing is impossible for us - nothing is unachievable for us - nothing is utopian for us.

But mark you, I am not saying that America is first in every achievement, for that would be a lie. Various cultures are first in various kinds of feats, and our America is first in exploration, at least in modern times that is. In the ancient times, several other civilizations used to be the first in terms of exploration and discovery, such as the ancient Indians, Arabs and Greeks, but as time passed the ominous cloud of intellectual pride engulfed these civilizations to such an extent that they lost their very original drive for exploration. Pride made them paralyzed and the new descendants of these civilizations became the very definition of mediocrity, with the exception of individual achievements.

That's why the oldest civilizations of the world are stagnating in terms of mental as well as material advancement, whereas despite being a rather young civilization, our America continues to carry the torch of progress ahead for all of humankind. And this puts us in a rather delicate position - a position of great significance as well as incomparable responsibility. It makes us accountable for not just our own fate but that of the whole of humankind.

You know why? Because any individual or nation that is in a position of power, is not only responsible for their own destiny, but also that of the fellow people. Blessed is the nation whose gospel is goodness and religion is service. Such is the character of a truly civilized nation - such is the character of a true civilization.

America was founded on the principle of life, liberty and the pursuit of happiness. Our motto has always been "home is where freedom is, community is where accountability is". And the integrity of a society is predicated on these two fundamentals - freedom and accountability. Freedom without accountability leads to chaos, accountability without freedom leads to nowhere.

3.   The New American Sonnet

The New American Sonnet

America doesn't mean the best,
America means accountability.
America doesn't mean supremacy,
America means responsible liberty.
America doesn't mean flawless,
America means growing against oddity.
America doesn't mean condescension,
America means caring for all humanity.
America doesn't mean white or color,
America means celebration of diversity.
America doesn't mean red or blue,
America means together crossing rigidity.
Stars and stripes have no place for hate.
Our heart is human, it's humanity we celebrate.

4.   Reaching For Humanhood

You can inherit riches, you can inherit status, you can inherit profession even, but you cannot inherit humanity - you have to earn it yourself by acting human. And if you choose not to act human, then you'd never attain humanhood - you are born an animal and you die an animal.

To raise a community it is imperative that we reach for humanhood in our individual lives, for when the individual turns human, the society turns human - or else we come from animals and we will remain animal till kingdom come. Therefore, it is imperative that in our individual life we act as if our life is the life of the collective, for it is. This very sense of collectivity in individuality is the definition of humanity.

You think it's food that keeps us alive! Let me tell you, it's not. It's not food that keeps us alive, it's unity. Starvation kills a body, but segregation kills a society. That's why, anybody who endorses division over unity is a terrorist. Segregation of any kind has no place in a civilized society, and when bigots forget this simple fact, they must be reminded of it, by the human beings of planet earth.

I am a child of earth, all this land is my home, and I won't allow any boneheaded bigot to divide my home. I have fought for three things all my life - my society, my humanity, my planet. Let everyone hear it - no matter the price, I won't stop till I unite the world or die trying. I was born of this earth, I fight for this earth, I'll merge into this earth. I promise, when one Naskar dies, a thousand Naskars will rise to take the place, for Naskar is not a person, it is a revolution. And there is no death for those who die for the people, there's only immortality.

5. **Healers Don't Exist**
(The Sonnet)

Healers Don't Exist
(The Sonnet)

Healers don't exist,
Only humans do.
Once you step outside the self,
You'll see the world anew.
Gods don't exist,
Only goodness does.
Prayers may soothe your soul,
Action is what change requires.
Psychics don't exist,
But sanctity is everywhere.
Once you stop conning your soul,
The bridge ahead will vividly appear.
When the heart awakens from superstition,
Everybody will be hometown human.

6.   No Future Without Integration

24

We will not kneel before the oppressor. We will not harm, we will not be violent, we will not turn into a mob, but we will not stand down either, we will not back down from our conviction. Who are we? We are the lovers of this land. Who are we? We are the children of this land. Who are we? We are the soldiers of this land. And we'll defend its honor, its serenity, its sanctity at all costs, even if it means putting ourselves in harm's way. I repeat, we won't resort to violence, but we won't back down either.

Let everyone hear it - we are radicals - we are radicals for love - we are radicals for inclusion - we are radicals for ascension. There is no change without radicalism. Dare to be a radical, but make sure it's for the right reason, for it takes very little for a reformer to turn into a terrorist. All great achievements of human history have been made by radicals, but at the same time, terrible acts of atrocity have also been committed by radicals. MLK was a radical, so was Hitler, but MLK was radical with the purpose of building an integrated society, whereas Hitler's goal was to build a segregated society.

Integration is the future, no matter who likes it or not. Without integration there is no future. But the very term integration is demeaning really. Why you ask? Because what is there to integrate? We are all people, then why does it surprise so many that people ought to stand together in their good times and bad! The day, we become so unified, that we forget the term integration, that'll be the real dawn of human civilization.

Beyond the labels of race, religion, gender and status, when the collective become the individual and the individual becomes the collective, that is the dawn of human civilization. And that future of an integrated world starts with an integrated community and an integrated community is born of an integrated heart.

7.   **Child of Earth**
(The Sonnet)

Child of Earth
(The Sonnet)

Walk, walk, walk ahead,
O brave child of earth.
Let no fear shackle your feet,
Selflessness paves all path.
Meditate on unity,
Dedicate to inclusion.
Educate your soul,
Be free from self-absorption.
Forget gender, religion and ideology,
Abolish all chains of tribalism.
Place people at your heart's altar,
One dream, one mission – universalism.
Shallow and separated we can stay no more.
We must break ourselves to let light outpour.

8. Conviction Shows The Way

The greatest love is the love for people. Where there is love, there is integration, where there is prejudice, there is degradation. And in our society the latter is more dominant whereas the former is considered an abnormality. That's the whole point of everything and that is the problem. And this must change. It's not complicated, it's this simple - we must make a choice, either integration or degradation.

You know why the world doesn't change, it's because most people end up being changed by the world instead of taking a stand for their conviction. Persuaded by insecurities they give in and conform to every single cockeyed whim of the world, lest they are seen as outcast or stupid.

Yesterday I was stupid, I wanted to change the world, today I am stupider still, so I am changing the world. The secret to changing the world is to concentrate all your powers on your conviction. The only way out of inhumanity is through our conviction of humanity. Your conviction will show the way, if you could just stand strong on it.

A lot of people will see you as enemy because of your conviction of inclusion and equality, but do not move an inch from your conviction, especially when the very fate of humanity is predicated on that conviction of yours. Let me tell you a story which my father used to tell me when I was a kid. There was once a reformer in Bengal, the place I was born in. One evening he was walking by the river with a friend of his. Suddenly someone at a distance started shouting at him using curse words. The friend asked - why is the man cursing you, aren't you going to say anything? The reformer replied, let them shout, it only means that perhaps I am actually bringing some change in the society.

So let the critics and haters shout as much as they want. Do not engage, just keep doing your work, keep walking in the direction of your conviction. You cannot speak of justice without offending the defenders of injustice - you cannot speak of equality without offending the advocates of exclusion - you cannot speak of reason without offending the tradesmen of superstition.

I do not engage with any statement that is meant as a trap and not as a gesture of genuine curiosity. When people have already made you an opponent in their mind, there is nothing you can say that can change their opinion. So it is futile to even engage with them. Use their comments to sharpen and strengthen your conviction, but make not the mistake of replying. And even if you do reply, the moment you recognize their contempt, retreat calmly from the conversation.

Human mind is never flawless, that's why every conviction it produces, is also never flawless. Therefore it is imperative that you keep working on your conviction, work on its flaws, make it stronger, make it sharper, make it less flawed by the day. Remember, the difference between a reformer and a bigot is that, a bigot never evolves, but a reformer evolves constantly - that's what enables a reformer to revolutionize the society. The reformer is the reform, the revolutionary is the revolution.

All reform starts with the individual, but only when the individual can feel the ambitions and sentiments of the entire collective within their chest. Change can be both good and bad - when that change improves lives, it's a reform, but when it vilifies life, it's degradation.

Forget isms and give all to society. Remember, the highest meditation is to stop meditating and start working for society. Better die a daring reformer than a cowardly conformer. The question never is, can you change the world, the question is, are you ready to die (not harm) trying to change the world.

9. The Ultimate Sanity

The stone-age world was made of darkness, a civilized world can't be so - a civilized world is made of light, the light that you hold inside. You see, the birthplace of the world is the human heart - the birthplace of civilization is the human heart. That's how we built our America, out of sheer will. We forged this country against impossible odds and made it one of the most powerful nations on earth.

Now the time has come to foster a hundred times more determination than that with which we are to build a civilized world of inclusion out of sheer will, both inside America and outside. How can we do that you ask? You are not part of civilization, you are the civilization - you are the seed of civilization, nourish yourself well with conscience, courage and compassion, and civilization will manifest all around you.

The point is, it's not about the prosperity of one country over the others - it is about the prosperity and progress of the whole of humankind. So, no matter where we are, we must aim towards making that corner of our society a living, breathing example of true civilization, from which the whole world can draw inspiration.

O Mighty Human, Lead, Kindly Light, for thy light is the world's might. Only the human heart can turn a savage world into a human one, not law, not government, not any authority of any kind. Justice springs out of the human heart alone - equality springs out of the human heart alone - integration springs out of the human heart alone.

Until the qualities of justice, equality and integration spring out of the hearts of the citizens of a nation, no matter how much we pretend to maintain the illusion of secularism and assimilation through legislative means, internally the country will remain conflicted till eternity. Therefore I say to you o braveheart - lose yourself in serving the people, for there's no other way.

Pay no heed to hate, have no care for competition, just give all to society. The sun's purpose is to give light, it knows no competition, it knows no hate. It just gives and gives and gives, and it still never says that the world owes it anything. It's a kind of a madness - it's a kind of a craziness - something that no sane, calculating, security-seeking savage can comprehend - it's the craziness for giving.

Yes, I am crazy - crazy for people. Without craziness there is no reform. Only with this craziness - only with this madness, will we take our world ahead. Only with our madness to lift the society, will we bring the ultimate sanity - the sanity of inclusivity - the sanity of oneness.

Remember, oneness alone is sanity, all else is insanity. Unity alone is serenity, divisiveness is insecurity. We have wasted enough time and energy on philosophical and intellectual debates over terminologies and definitions - we no longer have any time - it is time for work - it is time for action - we must work with our fullest potential towards the direction of oneness. And to do that we must become one with the rest of humanity.

We must become the living embodiment of oneness in our own life. And that one flame of oneness will light many more candles around - and soon enough all those little, apparently insignificant flames will turn into a grand, purifying torch of universal oneness - a torch for the light of which the entire sky will fall short.

Once we are one with the rest of humanity, there will neither be our America their America, nor our country their country - it'll be all ours. All you have to do is bring down the barriers - the barriers of intellect, ideology and culture. Become a freedom incarnate like our lady liberty, and the society will start to unify around you.

Work, don't define your work - work as the living manifestation of inclusion - work as the living manifestation of oneness - work as the living manifestation of the best of humankind, overpowering the worst of humanity within you by the force of your conscience. When you feel one, all the troubles of the world will appear as they are, your troubles - all the sufferings of the world will appear as they are, your sufferings. Indifference has no place in a civilized society. This very indifference is the cause of all the inequalities in the world.

With indifference people are continuously breeding a society full of disparity – they are constantly aiding the creation of more inequality. We are constantly making way for a world where some parents give their kids x-box to soothe them, for their birthday, and many more parents are forced to use leftover cardboard boxes as cradle for their babies because they don't even have a roof over their head. This is our so called civilization - this is our so called modern humanity - shame on us - shame on us as a species - shame on us as civilized beings - shame on us as thinking and breathing individuals of conscience. No more - no more - we must break this disparity - and we must do it right now - and we are not going to do it by fighting over whose ideology is the best - we are going to do it only by taking actual responsibility of our society - by taking actual responsibility of the world - we are going to do it by acting as a living cure for those disparities, by using our own resources as means to erase those gaps however we can. Only with action born from our heart can we end disparity, not with talks of argument and inaction of complacency.

10. In The Church of Liberty
(The Sonnet)

46

In The Church of Liberty
(The Sonnet)

In the church of liberty,
Light a candle of conviction.
Do not move an inch,
Even in the face of annihilation.
Freedom, curiosity and inclusivity,
These are the beads of our soul.
Standing true to these watchwords,
We will reach our supreme goal.
If we want there to be serenity,
Destroy we must our insane egotism.
Real rest comes through humility,
When we discover the self in collectivism.
World peace and harmony are all fiction.
If conscience is awake there'll be ascension.

11. When Liberty Calls

As I said earlier, every nation has a distinct backbone, ours is liberty, and we must stand up whenever that liberty is in jeopardy, be it on our shores or elsewhere, for liberty has no national identity, it only has one identity, the identity of humanity.

When liberty is in jeopardy in any nation of earth, it is our civilized responsibility as a capable people to be involved and right the wrong - we cannot refrain from engaging in the affairs of other nations, if those affairs continue to show signs of persecution, discrimination and an utter violation of human liberty. Violation of liberty in one nation is not that nation's internal business, it is the business of every conscientious and capable nation on earth, it is the business of every conscientious and capable individual on earth.

Let them call us big brother if they want - a civilized world is built by concerned and caring brothers and sisters, not by cold and indifferent strangers. We must safeguard life, liberty and happiness wherever they are threatened, without the slightest desire for conquest. Let everyone hear it, we have come to conquer hearts, not lands - we have come to erase misery, not identity - we have come to instill equality, not slavery.

Our motive makes the difference. We are capable, we are conscientious, we are courageous, that's enough reason for us to be involved in the affairs of every single community on earth whenever the need arises, for that is what humanity is all about, to take care of others in their time of need.

But again, we mustn't be involved too much - we mustn't help other nations to such an extent that they lose their faculty of self-reliance. As I have said in my previous works, the greatest help is to help someone become self-reliant. Keeping this in mind, we must stand tall as a pillar of liberty, accountability and reason for the whole world to draw courage from. This holds true not just for a capable country, but also for a capable human being.

It is the role of a capable heart to lift others up and make them capable enough to carve their own destiny. Remember, our purpose is to make the whole humankind capable - to make the whole humankind self-determined. It is our purpose, it is our promise - the promise of a responsible sentience - a sentience that never turns its back on a distressed neighbor – it is the promise of a people who never turn their back on a distressed community. If communities do not come to help each other in times of need, then what's the point of having a community – what's the point of having life!

12. In Humanity We Trust

A civilized world will grow out of our own heart, once we realize, there's no greater truth than the one of the heart - the heart which is neither black, nor white, the heart which is neither man, nor woman, nor non-binary, the heart which is neither wise nor foolish, the heart which is neither rich nor poor - the heart which is ever-free, ever-boundless.

Yet the unfortunate reality is, today's norms are born of bounds - bounds of culture, bounds of faith, bounds of intellect and so on. The situation is so dire that norms are often synonymous with bounds. This must change. If anything, norms ought to be synonymous with accountability, not bounds. And it can only change with you - you the individual. Norms ought to be the product of accountability and reason, not insecurity and superstition.

In a civilized society, the motto is, in humanity we trust, not god, law or party. In a civilized society, there is no faith or blasphemy, there is only people - in a civilized society, there is no fact or fiction, there is only people - in a civilized society, there is no minority or majority, there is only people. If you want to build a truly secular and civilized society, then you must throw away all nonsense of savage dualities, such as majority and minority. A civilized nation never uses terms like majority and minority to refer to people, it's only the uncivilized nation that does so. In people we'll find salvation.

Those who are arrogant about their pedigree, about their culture, about their intellect, I have no business with them, give me the humble janitor, give me the illiterate construction worker, give me the dropout waitress - the humble soul will find me in their own heart, but the arrogant will argue their whole life and never understand what I am all about, what humanity is all about - it's about community, it's about listening, it's about letting go of one's self-obsessed identity to become one with humanity. You see, when we loosen the knots of our identity in celebration of humanity, we not only become stronger as a people, but also our own identity expands beyond our wildest imagination.

The need of the hour is self-expansion, not self-absorption. Don't place barriers on your heart, let it expand - let it expand far and wide. One expanded heart makes a hundred more hearts expand. One ignited heart makes the whole humanity ignite.

The human heart is highly inflammable, but it's not facts that make the heart ignite, it's not intellect that makes the heart ignite, it's sentiments - sentiments without segregation, sentiments without sexism, sentiments without sectarianism.

13. My Compatriots
(The Sonnet)

62

My Compatriots
(The Sonnet)

Any compatriot of mine,
Better have a grasp of prejudice.
Arrogance sickens my soul,
My heart revolts at the snobbish.
Doubts can be healthy,
But only if driven by curiosity.
When driven by contempt,
They only facilitate animosity.
You don't have to agree,
With the whole of my notion.
But don't turn bitter my friend,
For it is a trap of degradation.
Logic may fail sometimes as well as sentiments.
Never you lose o patriot your indivisible humanness.

14. Live By Ideas, Not Labels

Why should there be barriers on the heart! The heart beats the same way, no matter the geography, both the metaphorical and the physiological heart. Its purpose is the same, no matter the culture - to energize an anatomy, to empower an individual. And a heart that is capable of empowering an individual, can empower an entire world. That's how we are to build the civilization, by being the cause of it. That's how we are to build the future, by causing the future.

Every accountable human being is the future in action. Every reformer is the future in action. Every revolutionary is the future in action. But no reformer ever stops to consider themselves as reformer, they just do what's the human thing to do, and that's all. And that is the role of a human being. Political analysts and philosophers may call us reformers, but never forget my bravehearts, the life of a human requires no intellectual label.

Kids live by labels, grownups live by ideas. And when you live by labels, at some point if you get angry enough, you'll end up resorting to violence - you'll end up resorting to guns. So, by living by labels you are soon going to end up living by guns. And leeches live by guns, legends live by ideas. Owning a gun doesn't increase civilian security, it only threatens it, thus making it far more difficult for law enforcement to ensure public safety.

It is this simple, law enforcement exists to ensure the safety of the public, but if the public are primitive enough to think that all they need to ensure their safety is a personal firearm, then we better destroy all things civilized and head back to the jungle, because a society where anybody can own a gun is not a society, but a jungle anyways.

Here our intellect may argue - can ideas not do harm as well - what about those extremists who are driven by their idea of ancestral, cultural or religious supremacy - don't they do harm, living by ideas! And when we look at it that way, then the answer that appears is one - ideas that do harm are no ideas, they are delusion. Ideas ought to breathe life - ideas ought to facilitate growth - ideas ought to inspire curiosity and harmony - failing to do so, an idea fails to be an idea and exists as yet another product of biases and prejudices.

There are always two ways to look at ideas. One is to look at them as concepts of books and another is to look at them as part of life. For example, in America we call it "elevator", in Britain we call it "lift", but the thing is the same. Likewise, some people call it science, some philosophy, others religion, I call it life, I call it humanity. In practice, there is no divide among the three. They are one intertwined, inseparable organism of ascension. So, our ideas may appear different on the outside, but in practice their goal is the same, it's ascension.

15. Common Sense Civilization

Once you feel the force of humanity course through your veins, no amount of comfort and luxury can keep you from being restless at the sight of human misery. Why doesn't your blood boil - why doesn't it boil for society - is there blood or ice water in your veins - if there is blood in your veins, then you won't be able to sit still when the entire humankind is suffering from sectarianism, bigotry and disparity - if there is blood in your veins that very blood will direct your every thought in the line of service - in the course of upliftment - but I guess it's indeed ice water that flows through your veins, that's why you are silent - that's why you are sleeping - that's why you stay cooped up in insecurity - doesn't this make you bothered - doesn't' this make you rise from your couch and shout out to the world - my veins carry blood - the blood of a human, and I won't stay silent - I won't stay asleep - I won't stay insecure - here I stand, trampling all insecurity - insecurity that is not mine, but those of my environment - here I stand - as a human being - with an upright spine and firm conviction - I stand on guard to defend the people, and I'll die with a smile on my face protecting the integrity of the fabric of humanity rather than giving in to the whims of the self-obsessed, opportunist, snobbish, moronic and monstrous masses. I am free, I am accountable and I will die a heroic death for my conviction, rather than living a life of an insect for no reason.

Without a handful of headstrong humans standing strong on the conviction of inclusion, reason and ascension, the river of humanity will dry out in a matter of days. But I repeat, violence has no place in a civilized society, and more importantly in a civilized revolution. If you think something in your society is not right, then the right path is to just stand unbending on your conviction of humanity and not move till you see the society change its course from its self-righteous savage direction to a self-correcting humane direction.

Remember, what is inside, is also outside, for the outside is only a reflection of the inside. So if there is real unity inside you, the world is bound to be united - but if the world is not united, look for the cause nowhere else but inside. If there is light, a human is the reason, if there is darkness, a human is the reason. If there is unity, a human is the reason, if there is division, a human is the reason.

It is our world and our world is our reflection, that is - the human world is a reflection of the human - the individual human, for the collective starts with the individual – the whole of humanity starts with the individual human.

It's not about being a republican or a democrat - it's not about being a conservative or a liberal - it's not about being a catholic or a humanist - it's not about being a capitalist or a communist - it's about your ability to distinguish humanity from inhumanity - it's about your ability to distinguish harmony from disharmony - it's about your ability to distinguish science from conspiracy - it's about your ability to distinguish accountability from savagery.

You don't need to be a highly educated scholar or a brilliant scientist to distinguish these, common sense would suffice. And if you can practice that common sense to distinguish all that is civilized from all that is primitive, then you can be whatever you want, it won't affect your humanity the least bit - then you no longer have to worry about the so-called political correctness or party loyalty.

As I said, there is no our America their America, there is only one America, the United States of America. There is no our world their world, there is only one world, the human world. Likewise, there is no our culture their culture, there is only one culture, the human culture.

This doesn't mean that you have to erase all traces of attachment to the culture you are born in - in fact, no matter how much you try, you can never do that, because by the time you grow up, certain cultural elements get indelibly chiseled in your brain circuits. The only thing that is required of you is that you don't become a prisoner of your culture.

For example, America is my motherland, not because I was born here, but because this is the land that adopted me as a son when nobody knew I exist, so obviously I will always have an unparalleled attachment to my land of liberty, but that doesn't mean that I am the exclusive possession of any single culture. Naskar lives in every culture, Naskar belongs to every culture. Different cultures may call me differently, but the force is universal.

If you pour some water from the river into a glass and call it glass-water, does it stop being the river - it still remains the river - likewise, you may call my ideas differently - some call it humanism, some humanitarianism, some socialism, some sufism and others nondualism, but at the end of the day, the ideas remain the same - they are just plain, ordinary ideas of an indivisible and accountable humanity.

16. Cure for Disparities

The world has plenty room for everyone, once we spread our heart wide as the world and make our desires thin as a pin. Desire beyond necessity is the cause of all disparities. A responsible human ought to engage in the gratification of desire only to the point of sustaining the body and mind - accomplishing that, rest of the human potential should go to acts of growth, both personal and social.

In fact, in a civilized society there is no separation between personal and social, they are one and the same - what's social must be personal, what's personal must be social - only then can we build a healthy and serene society. And for that you must feel the troubles of your society in your bones like salt on a wound. If you can do that my friend, then ascension is assured, both for you and your society. When the human is ready, civilization will appear.

I burnt my youth, so that you could have a torch. Take this torch and ignite yourself - burn my soldier of ascension, burn - the more you burn, the more human this world will become. Nothing can put this fire out – nothing must - the day it goes out, is the day the world runs out of humanity.

One person can change the fate of a country - one person can change the fate of a planet - all that is needed is to burn till death. The fire of sacrifice is the cure for all the troubles in the world - this fire is the cure for all the darkness in the world - this fire is the cure for all the inhumanity in the world.

The heart breeds sickness, the heart holds the cure. We are the sickness, we are the cure. Throw all insecurity overboard and be the cure for this sick world of ours however you can. Even the tiniest effort counts. As I have said in my previous works, it's not the size of your step that counts, it's the intention behind it.

If you do even one simple deed with the genuine intention of benefiting the society, it is bound to inspire an uplifting change in the world. A genuine society starts with a genuine intention for betterment. If an intention is genuine, then that very intention will produce action, which in turn will produce results. Lack of change is not a sign of misfortune, it's a sign of inaction.

So if we want a united world - a world where diversity is the reason for celebration, not a cause for prejudice, we must have the desire for such a world - we must yearn for such a world as a thirsty traveler in the desert yearns for water. If the yearning is genuine, the road will appear.

17. Goodbye Mother
(The Sonnet)

Goodbye Mother
(The Sonnet)

Bid me goodbye o mother,
Be right back once I plant unity.
If I do not return from my journey,
Soothe yourself knowing I've died happily.
These rusted shackles hurt too much,
It's time o mother to abolish them forever.
Shoulder to shoulder your children will walk,
At the sight of our conviction bigots will quiver.
The sacred river of life has long gone dry,
I'll resuscitate it with my blood and integrity.
Your children are my family o mother,
With my last breath I will fortify their destiny.
Bless me o mother of all for my mission awaits.
I'll return victorious or die a martyr's death.

18. Founding A United Earth

While walking in the course of your passion, starve your rigidity and feed your morality. Keep working on your morality - keep working on your conscience - keep working on your righteousness - stop not, no matter what. You are not at your best –we are never at our best – there's always room for improvement, there's always room for evolution – so keep working on yourself – ever-learning – ever-growing.

And when your feet bleed from walking, that's when the wounds of the world are healed. We can heal the world only when we are willing to bleed ourselves for the world. Only when we stand unafraid to bleed all over our being with a genuine, unconflicted, uncorrupted, unselfish desire for good, will we be the founder of a civilized planet.

Gone are the days when we can stupidly think of the security of one nation alone - gone are the days when we can nationalistically care for one nation over all others - whatever we do today we must do it with the ultimate goal to benefit the whole of humanity, not just a small primitive tribe.

You will not know me as the father of a nation, you will know me as a founder of the united earth. I envision a valley, beyond red and blue, beyond flags and barbwires, beyond capitols and churches, where our descendants will sit together around a campfire and tell each other stories of the olden days - "remember when our ancestors used to live in tribes - they called it religion, nation, race and all that - how silly right!" I work towards that future. And so must you, no matter how you do it, because the very destiny of humankind hangs on your action.

You are the universe - never forget that - what's one civilization - you can build a hundred civilizations if you want to. It's all in the desire - it's all in the intention. How headstrong are you towards that goal - how heartstrong are you towards that goal, that's the question.

19. When Head and Heart Become One

There is this apparent divide between the head and the heart, which we must erase right away. In a whole and humane society, the heart is not just a symposium of sentiments, but it is also where reason resides, which means it is also where the head resides. If we are to move forward as an unprejudiced and inclusive lifeform, we cannot entertain the ancient conflict between logicality and sentimentality, we must advance with warmth as our identity and reason as our tool.

Prejudice is grounded on sentiments, that's where reason must intervene, and coldness is grounded on logic, that's where warmth must prevail. To achieve this you must observe everything as a human being standing on the ground of humanity - not as an intellectual or a sentimental, but as a plain, ordinary, everyday human being.

A better society begins with a firm grasp of prejudices. But what we must remember here is that no prejudice ever manifests as an obvious and harmful act, they always appear as harmless and common human sentiment. And that's where the trouble begins. They may be part of common human experience, but they are nowhere near harmless, that is, when we are talking about their existence in a civilized society and not in the jungle.

During our primitive days prejudices kept us divided and thus kept those small communities of savages up on their toes against possible invasions from each other. But such tribalism of our savage days is incompatible in an integrated world.

To put it simply, no matter how life was in our savage days, in our modern times life united elevates all of us, but life divided degrades all of us. And once you bring down the barriers imposed on you by your culture as well as by evolutionary primitiveness, the majesty of an indivisible life manifests through every step you take and every word you utter - a life that belongs everywhere and calls everyone its own - a life that finds a home wherever it goes.

I am a hometown human to every person in the world - every neighborhood is my neighborhood - every city is my city - every county is my county - every continent is my continent. And when enough humans on earth feel that the whole world is their home, hence their responsibility, no inhumanity will be strong enough to persist even a day.

20. Together We Are Beautiful

Inhumanity thrives on indifference - no indifference, no inhumanity. Sectarianism, discrimination, prejudice, all these thrive on indifference. Therefore, to eliminate these from the face of our planet, every last trace of indifference is to be replaced with accountability. Every individual with an alive conscience must turn into a patriot for this whole world, only then the countries of planet earth will actually turn human, be it our America or any other. Like all other countries, our stars and stripes have a lot of stains on it, and it'll take centuries of determined accountability to clean them off.

If we are to consider ourselves civilized, then as a country, we must act as the reflection of other countries, and other countries will act as the reflection of us, for all of humankind are the reflection of the individual human, and the individual human is the reflection of all humankind. Together we are alive and beautiful, divided we are dead and rotten.

We are reflections of each other - we belong to each other - the day you realize this, is the day you'll know life. This is the reason I don't adhere to any ideology - life is too grand to be bound by any single ideology - life is too sacred to be vilified by ideologies. Ideologies may have traces of life in them, and there is nothing wrong in embracing those traces when they amplify your capacity as a human, but you must never place ideologies before life.

Metaphorically speaking, the moment you were born as a human is the moment you were chosen by Nature to change the world, for no other creature on earth among 8.7 million species has the actual biological capacity to build a civilization – therefore, the question is, what will you die as - a fulfilled human or a wasted animal!

No brain can write poetry but the human brain - no brain can build rockets but the human brain - no brain can compose music but the human brain - with so much unparalleled potential tucked inside our head, most humans spend their lifetime on puny arguments over which color is better, which religion is better, which nation is better, which gender is better and so on. For once, if you could put aside all this savage nonsense, then we could achieve five hundred years of accomplishment in a single year.

A human mind that has a hold over its prejudices is like the fabled philosopher's stone, everything it touches turns to gold, whereas a savage mind which is run by its prejudices is like an infectious disease, wherever it goes it causes death and destruction.

BIBLIOGRAPHY

Archer M., (2000), Being Human: The Problem of Agency. Cambridge University Press.

Archer M., (2003), Structure, Agency and the Internal Conversation. Cambridge University Press.

Adolphs R (2003) Cognitive neuroscience of human social behaviour. Nature Rev Neurosci 4: 165–178.

Adolphs R, Tranel D, Damasio AR (2003) Dissociable neural systems for recognizing emotions. Brain Cogn 52: 61–69.

Afton, A. D. (1985). Forced copulation as a reproductive strategy of male lesser scaup: A field test of some predictions. - Behaviour 92, p. 146-167.

Allison T, Puce A, McCarthy G. (2000) Social perception from visual cues: role of the STS region. Trends Cogn Sci 4: 267–278.

Andresen, Jensine, and Robert Forman, eds. Cognitive Models and Spiritual Maps. Bowling Green, Ohio: Imprint Academic, 2000.

Ashbrook, James, and Carol Albright. The Humanizing Brain: Where Religion and Neuroscience Meet. Cleveland, OH: Pilgrim Press, 1997.

Azari, Nina, Janpeter Nickel, Gilbert Wunderlich, Michael Niedeggen, Harald Hefter, Lutz Tellmann, Hans Herzog, Petra Stoerig, Dieter Birnbacher, and Rudiger Seitz. "Neural Correlates of Religious Experience." European Journal of Neuroscience 13, no. 8 (2001)

Agar, N. (2004). Liberal eugenics: In defence of human enhancement. London: Blackwell Publishing.

Alteheld, N., Roessler, G., Vobig, M., & Walter, R. (2004). The retina implant new approach to a visual prosthesis. Biomedizinische Technik, 49(4), 99–103.

Antal, A., Nitsche, M. A., Kincses, T. Z., Kruse, W., Hoffmann, K. P., & Paulus, W. (2004a). Facilitation of visuo-motor learning by transcranial direct current stimulation of the motor and extrastriate visual areas in humans. European Journal of Neuroscience, 19(10), 2888–2892.

Bhat Z, Kumar, S, Bhat H (2015) In vitro meat production. Challenges and benefits over conventional meat production. J Sci Food Agric 14: 241–248

Bernstein R. J., (1967), John Dewey. New York: Washington Square Press.

Bernstein R.J., (1971), Praxis and Action: Contemporary Philosophies of Human Activity. Philadelphia: University of Pennsylvania Press.

Bernstein R.J., (1976), The Restructuring Social and Political Thought.

Bernstein R.J., (1983), Beyond Relativism and Objectivism: Science, Hermeneutics, and Praxis. Philadelphia: University of Pennsylvania Press.

Bernstein R.J., (1986), Philosophical Profiles. Philadelphia: University of Pennsylvania Press.

Bernstein R.J., (1991), New Constellation. Cambridge: MIT Press.

Barash, D. P. (1977). Sociobiology of rape in mallards (Anas platyrhynchos): Responses of the mated male. - Science 197, p. 788-789.

Berger, J. (1986). Wild horses of the great basin: Social competition and population size. - The University of Chicago Press, Chicago.

Birkhead, T. R., Johnson, S. D. & Nettleship, D. N. (1985). Extra-pair matings and mate guarding in the common murre Uria aalge. - Anim. Behav. 33, p. 608-619.

Beauregard, Mario, and Vincent Paquette. "Neural Correlates of a Mystical Experience in Carmelite Nuns." Neuroscience Letters 405, no. 3 (2006)

Benson, Herbert. Timeless Healing: The Power and Biology of Belief. New York: Scribner, 1996

Bogen, J.E.(1995a), 'On the neurophysiology of consciousness: Part I. An overview', Consciousness and Cognition, 4.

Bogen, J.E. (1995b), 'On the neurophysiology of consciousness: Part II. Constraining the semantic problem', Consciousness and Cognition, 4.

Bremner, J. D., R. Soufer, et al. (2001). "Gender differences in cognitive and neural correlates of remembrance of emotional words." Psychopharmacol Bull 35 (3).

Brothers, L. (2002). The social brain: A project for integrating primate behavior and neurophysiology in a new domain. In J. T. Cacioppo et al. (Eds.), Foundations in neuroscience. Cambridge, MA: MIT Press.

Buss, D. D. (2003). Evolutionary Psychology: The New Science of Mind, 2nd ed. New York: Allyn & Bacon.

Buss, D. M. (1989). "Conflict between the sexes: Strategic interference and the evocation of anger and upset." J Pers Soc Psychol 56 (5).

Buss, D. M. (1995). "Psychological sex differences. Origins through sexual selection." Am Psychol 50 (3).

Buss, D. M. (2002). "Review: Human Mate Guarding." Neuro Endocrinol Lett 23 (Suppl 4).

Buss, D. M., and D. P. Schmitt (1993). "Sexual strategies theory: An evolutionary perspective on human mating." Psychol Rev 100 (2).

Blakemore SJ, Decety J (2001) From the perception of action to the understanding of intention. Nature Rev Neurosci 2: 561.

Bruce C, Desimone R, Gross CG (1981) Visual properties of neurons in a polysensory area in superior temporal sulcus of the macaque. J Neurophysiol 46: 369–384.

Buccino G, Vogt S, Ritzl A, Fink GR, Zilles K, Freund HJ, Rizzolatti G (2004) Neural circuits underlying imitation of hand actions: an event related fMRI study. Neuron 42: 323–34.

Colapietro V., (1988), "Human Agency: The Habits of Our Being."

Southern Journal of Philosophy, XXVI, 2, pp. 153-68.

Colapietro V., (1992), "Purpose, Power, and Agency." The Monist, 75, 4 (October) pp. 423-44.

Colapietro V., (2003), "Signs and their vicissitudes: Meanings in excess of consciousness and functionality." Logica, Dialogica, Ideologica, a cure di Susan Petrilli e Patrizia Calefato (Milano: Mimesis), pp. 221-36.

Colapietro V., (2004a), "C. S. Peirce's Reclamation of Teleology." Nature in American Philosophy, ed. Jean De Groot (Washington, D.C.: Catholic University Press of America), pp. 88-108.

Colapietro V., (2004b), "Portrait of a Historicist: An Alternative Reading of Peircean Semiotic." Semiotiche, 2/04 [maggio 2004], pp. 49-68.

Colapietro V., (2006), "Engaged Pluralism: Between Alterity and

Sociality." The Pragmatic Century: Conversations with Richard J. Bernstein (Albany, NY: SUNY Press), pp. 39-68.

Colapietro V., (2009), "Habit, Competence, and Purpose." Forthcoming in The Transactions of the Charles S. Peirce Society. Calder AJ, Keane J, Manes F, Antoun N, Young AW (2000) Impaired recognition and experience of disgust following brain injury. Nature Neurosci 3: 1077–1078.

Carey DP, Perrett DI, Oram MW (1997) Recognizing, understanding and reproducing actions. In: Jeannerod M, Grafman J (eds) Handbook of neuropsychology. Vol. 11: Action and cognition. Elsevier, Amsterdam.

Carr L, Iacoboni M, Dubeau MC, Mazziotta JC, Lenzi GL (2003) Neural mechanisms of empathy in humans: a relay from neural systems for imitation to limbic areas. Proc Natl Acad Sci USA 100: 5497–5502.

Changeux JP, Ricoeur P (1998) La nature et la règle. Odile Jacob, Paris.

Cochin S, Barthelemy C, Roux S, Martineau J (1999) Observation and execution of movement: similarities demonstrated by quantified electroencephalograpy. Eur J Neurosci 11: 1839– 1842.

Chomsky Noam, (2017) Requiem for the American Dream

Chomsky Noam, (2016) Who Rules the World?

Chomsky Noam, (2010) How the World Works

Churchland, P.S. (1986), Neurophilosophy (Cambridge, MA: The MIT Press).

Churchland, P.S. & Ramachandran, V.S. (1993), 'Filling in: Why Dennett is wrong', in Dennett and His Critics:

Demystifying Mind, ed. B. Dahlbom (Oxford: Blackwell Scientific Press).

Churchland, P.S., Ramachandran, V.S. & Sejnowski, T.J. (1994), 'A critique of pure vision', in Large- scale Neuronal Theories of the Brain, ed. C. Koch & J.L. Davis (Cambridge, MA: The MIT Press).

Crick, F. (1994), The Astonishing Hypothesis: The Scientific Search for the Soul (New York: Simon and Schuster).

Crick, F. (1996), 'Visual perception: rivalry and consciousness', Nature, 379.

Crick, F. & Koch, C. (1992), 'The problem of consciousness', Scientific American, 267.

Craig AD (2002) How do you feel? Interoception: the sense of the physiological condition of the body. Nature Rev Neurosci 3: 655–666.

Damasio, A (2003a) Looking for Spinoza. Harcourt Inc. Damasio A (2003b) Feeling of emotion and the self. Ann NY Acad Sci 1001: 253–261.

d'Aquili, Eugene. "Senses of Reality in Science and Religion." Zygon 17, no 4 (1982)

d'Aquili, Eugene. "The Biopsychological Determinants of Religious Ritual Behavior." Zygon 10, no. 1 (1975)

d'Aquili, Eugene. "The Myth-Ritual Complex: A Biogenetic Structural Analysis." Zygon 18, no. 3 (1983)

d'Aquili, Eugene, and Andrew Newberg. The Mystical Mind: Probing the Biology of Religious Experience. Minneapolis: Fortress Press, 1999.

Daly DD. 1958. Ictal affect. Am J Psychiatry.

Damasio, A. (1994) Descartes' Error: Emotion, Reason and the Human Brain. New York, Putnams.

Damasio, A. (1999) The Feeling of What Happens: Body, Emotion and the Making of Consciousness. London, Heinemann.

Darwin, C. (1859) On the Origin of Species by Means of Natural Selection. London, Murray.

Darwin, C. (1871) The Descent of Man and Selection in Relation to Sex. London, John Murray.

Darwin, C. (1872) The Expression of the Emotions in Man and Animals. London, John Murray; also published 1965, Chicago, University of Chicago Press.

Dawkins, M.S. (1987) Minding and mattering. In C. Blakemore and S. Greenfield (eds) Mindwaves. Oxford, Blackwell, 151-60.

Dawkins, R. (1976) The Selfish Gene. Oxford, Oxford University Press; a new edition, with additional material, was published in 1989.

Dawkins, R. (1986) The Blind Watchmaker. London, Longman.

Di Pellegrino G, Fadiga L, Fogassi L, Gallese V, Rizzolatti G (1992) Understanding motor events: A neurophysiological study. Exp Brain Res 91: 176–80.

Deikman, A.J. (2000) A functional approach to mysticism. Journal of Consciousness Studies 7(11-12), 75-91.

Delmonte, M.M. (1987) Personality and meditation. In M. West (ed.) The Psychology of Meditation. Oxford, Clarendon Press, 118-32.

Dennett, D.C. (1987) The Intentional Stance. Cambridge, MA, MIT Press.

Dennett, D.C. (1988) Quining qualia. In A.J. Marcel and E. Bisiach (eds)

Consciousness in Contemporary Science. Oxford, Oxford University Press, 42-77.

Dennett, D.C. (1991) Consciousness Explained. Boston, MA, and London, Little, Brown and Co.

Dennett, D.C. (1995a) Darwin's Dangerous Idea. London, Penguin.

Dennett, D.C. (1995b) The unimagined preposterousness of zombies. Journal of Consciousness Studies 2(4), 322-6.

Dennett, D.C. (1995c) Cog: steps towards consciousness in robots. In T. Metzinger (ed.) Conscious Experience. Thorverton, Devon, Imprint Academic, 471-87.

Dennett, D.C. (1995d) The path not taken. Behavioral and Brain Sciences 18, 252-3; commentary on N. Block, On a confusion about a function of consciousness. Behavioral and Brain Sciences 18, 227.

Dennett, D.C. (1996a) Facing backwards on the problem of consciousness. Journal of Consciousness Studies 3(1), 4-6.

Dennett, D.C. (1996b) Kinds of Minds: Towards an Understanding of Consciousness. London, Weidenfeld & Nicolson.

Dennett, D.C. (1997) An exchange with Daniel Dennett. In J. Searle (ed.) The Mystery of Consciousness. New York, New York Review of Books, 115-19.

Dennett, D.C. (1998) The myth of double transduction. In S.R. Hameroff, A.W. Kaszniak and A. C. Scott (eds) Toward a Science of Consciousness: The Second Tucson Discussions and Debates. Cambridge, MA, MIT Press, 97-107.

Dennett, D.C. (1998b) Brainchildren: Essays on Designing Minds. Cambridge, MA, MIT Press.

Dennett, D.C. (2001) The fantasy of first person science. Debate with D. Chalmers, Northwestern University, Evanston, IL, February 2001.

Dennett, D.C. (2003) Freedom Evolves. New York, Penguin.

Dennett, D.C. and Kinsbourne, M. (1992) Time and the observer: the where and when of consciousness in the brain. Behavioral and Brain Sciences 15, 183-247, including commentaries and authors' responses.

Dewey J., (1911 [1977]), "Epistemological Realism: The Alleged Ubiquity of the Knowledge Relation." Journal of Philosophy, VIII, 20 (September 28, 1911).

Dewhurst, Kenneth, and A. W. Beard. "Sudden Religious Conversions in Temporal Lobe Epilepsy." British Journal of Psychiatry 117 (1970)

Dewhurst K, Beard AW. Sudden religious conversions in temporal lobe epilepsy. 1970 Epilepsy Behav 2003

Devinsky O, Lai G. Spirituality and religion in epilepsy. Epilepsy Behav 2008.

Devinsky, O., Morrell, MJ, Vogt, BA. (1995) 'Contribution of anterior cingulate cortex to behavior', Brain, 118.

Douglas Stone A., Chapter 24, The Indian Comet, in the book Einstein and the Quantum, Princeton University Press, Princeton, New Jersey, 2013.

E. Horvitz, "One Hundred Year Study on Artificial Intelligence: Reflections and Framing," ed: Stanford University, 2014.

Einstein A. (1925). "Quantentheorie des einatomigen idealen Gases". Sitzungsberichte der Preussischen Akademie der Wissenschaften.

Eckhart Meister, Selected Writings

Egidi R., ed. (1999), "Von Wright and 'Dante's Dream': Stages in a Philosophical Pilgrim's Progress", in In Search of a New Humanism: the Philosophy of G.H. von Wright, ed. by R. Egidi, Kluwer, Dordrecht.

Fadiga L, Fogassi L, Pavesi G, Rizzolatti G (1995) Motor facilitation during action observation: a magnetic stimulation study. J Neurophysiol 73: 2608–2611.

Fogassi L, Gallese V, Fadiga L, Rizzolatti G (1998) Neurons responding to the sight of goal directed hand/arm actions in the parietal area PF (7b) of the macaque monkey. Soc Neurosci Abs 24:257.5.

Frith U, Frith CD (2003) Development and neurophysiology of mentalizing. Philos Trans R Soc Lond B Biol Sci 358: 459.

Farah, M.J. (1989), 'The neural basis of mental imagery', Trends in Neurosciences, 10.

Finlay BL, Darlington RB (1995) Linked regularities in the development and evolution of mammalian brains. Science 268.

Freud, S. "The Interpretation of Dreams", 1900

Freud, S. "Selected papers on hysteria and other psychoneuroses" Journal of Nervous and Mental Disease 1909.

Freud, S. "The Origin and Development of Psychoanalysis", 1910

Freud, S. "Psychopathology of everyday life", 1914

Freud, S. "Beyond the Pleasure Principle", 1920

Frith, C.D. & Dolan, R.J. (1997), 'Abnormal beliefs: Delusions and memory', Paper presented at the May,

1997, Harvard Conference on Memory and Belief.

Gay, Volney, ed. Neuroscience and Religion. Plymouth, UK: Lexington Books, 2009.

Gazzaniga, M. S. (1985). The social brain. New York: Basic Books.

Gazzaniga, M.S. (1993), 'Brain mechanisms and conscious experience', Ciba Foundation Symposium, 174.

Geschwind N. "Behavioural changes in temporal lobe epilepsy". Psychol Med. 1979.

Gellhorn, E., Kiely, W.F. "Mystical states of consciousness: neurophysiological and clinical aspects." J Nerv Ment Dis. 1972;154:399-405.

Gilbert SL, Dobyns WB, Lahn BT (2005) Genetic links between brain development and brain evolution. Nat Rev Genet 6.

Gray JA. The Psychology of Fear and Stress. 2nd ed. New York, NY: Cambridge University Press; 1988.

Gloor, P. (1992), 'Amygdala and temporal lobe epilepsy', in The Amygdala: Neurobiological Aspects of Emotion, Memory and Mental Dysfunction, ed J.P. Aggleton (New York: Wiley-Liss).

Greenspan, S. I. and S. G. Shanker (2004). The first idea: How symbols, language, and intelligence evolved from our early primate ancestors to modern humans. Cambridge, MA: Da Capo Press.

Grady, D. (1993), 'The vision thing: Mainly in the brain', Discover, June.

Gallagher HL, Frith CD (2003) Functional imaging of 'theory of mind'. Trends Cogn Sci 7: 77.

Gallese V, Fogassi L, Fadiga L, Rizzolatti G (2002) Action representation and the inferior parietal lobule. In: Prinz W, Hommel B (eds) Attention & Performance XIX. Common mechanisms in perception and action. Oxford University Press, Oxford.

Gallese V, Keysers C, Rizzolatti G (2004) A unifying view of the basis of social cognition. Trends Cogn Sci 8: 396–403.

Gangitano M, Mottaghy FM, Pascual-Leone A (2001) Phase specific modulation of cortical motor output during movement observation. NeuroReport 12: 1489–1492.

Gangitano M, Mottaghy FM, Pascual-Leone A (2004) Modulation of premotor mirror neuron activity during observation of unpredictable grasping movements. Eur J Neurosci 20: 2193– 2202.

Goldman AI, Sripada CS (2004) Simulationist models of face-based emotion recognition. Cognition 94: 193–213.

Grèzes J, Costes N, Decety J (1998) Top-down effect of strategy on the perception of human biological motion: a PET investigation. Cogn Neuropsychol 15: 553–582.

Grèzes J, Armony JL, Rowe J, Passingham RE (2003) Activations related to "mirror" and "canonical" neurones in the human brain: an fMRI study. Neuroimage 18: 928–937.

Gross CG, Rocha-Miranda CE, Bender DB (1972) Visual properties of neurons in the inferotemporal cortex of the macaque. J Neurophysiol 35: 96–111.

Hari R, Forss N, Avikainen S, Kirveskari S, Salenius S, Rizzolatti G (1998) Activation of human primary motor cortex during action observation: a neuromagnetic study.

Proc. Natl Acad Sci USA 95: 15061–15065.

Hardy, G. H. (1940). Ramanujan. Cambridge: Cambridge University Press.

Hall, Daniel, Keith Meador, and Harold Koenig. "Measuring Religiousness in Health Research: Review and Critique." Journal of Religion and Health 47, no. 2 (2008)

Harris, Sam, Jonas Kaplan, Ashley Curiel, Susan Bookheimer, Marco Iacoboni, and Mark Cohen. "The Neural Correlates of Religious and Nonreligious Belief." PLoS One 4, no. 10 (October 1, 2009)

Halgren, E. (1992), 'Emotional neurophysiology of the amygdala within the context of human cognition', in The Amygdala: Neurobiological Aspects of Emotion, Memory and Mental Dysfunction, ed J.P. Aggleton (New York: Wiley-Liss).

Halligan PW, Fink GR, Marshal JC, Vallar G. 2003. Spatial cognition: evidence from visual neglect. Trends Cogn Sci.

Handbook of Emotions, Edited by Michael Lewis, Jeannette M. Haviland-Jones, and Lisa Feldman Barrett, The Guilford Press; 3rd edition (2010).

Haggard, P., Clark, S. and Kalogeras,]. (2002) Voluntary action and conscious awareness, Nature Neuroscience 5, 382-5. Haggard, P., Newman, C. and Magno, E. (1999) On the perceived time of voluntary actions. British Journal of Psychology 90, 291-303.

Hameroff, S.R. and Penrose, R. (1996) Conscious events as orchestrated space-time selections. Journal of Consciousness Studies 3(1), 36-53; also reprinted in J. Shear (ed.) (1997) Explaining Consciousness-The Hard Problem. Cambridge, MA, MIT Press, 177-95.

Hardcastle, V.G. (2000) How to understand theN in NCC. InT. Metzinger (ed.) Neural Correlates of Consciousness. Cambridge, MA, MIT Press, 259-64.

Harding, D.E. (1961) On Having no Head: Zen and the Re-Discovery of the Obvious. London, Buddhist Society.

Hardy, A. (1979) The Spiritual Nature of Man: A Study of Contemporary Religious Experience. Oxford, Clarendon Press.

Hamad, S. (1990) The symbol grounding problem. Physica D 42, 335-46.

Hamad, S. (2001) No easy way out. The Sciences 41(2), 36-42.

Harre, R. and Gillett, G. (1994) The Discursive Mind. Thousand Oaks, CA, Sage.

Haugeland, J. (ed.) (1997) Mind Design II: Philosophy, Psychology, Artificial

Intelligence. Cambridge, MA, MIT Press.

Hauser, M.D. (2000) Wild Minds: What Animals Really Think. New York, Henry Holt and Co.; London, Penguin.

Hearne, K. (1990) The Dream Machine. Northants, Aquarian.

Hebb, D.O. (1949) The Organization of Behavior. New York, Wiley.

Helmholtz, H.L.F. von (1856-67) Treatise on Physiological Optics.

Hess, EH (1975) "The role of pupil size in communication," Scientific American, 233(5), 110–12.

Heyes, C.M. (1998) Theory of mind in nonhuman primates. Behavioral and Brain Sciences 21, 101-48; with commentaries.

Heyes, C.M. and Galef, B.G. (eds) (1996) Social Learning in Animals: The Roots of Culture. San Diego, CA, Academic Press.

Hilgard, E.R. (1986) Divided Consciousness: Multiple Controls in Human Thought and Action. New York, Wiley.

Hitler Adolf, "Mein Kampf", 1925

Hocquette JF (2016) Is in vitro meat the

solution for the future? Meat Science 120:

167–176

Hodgson, R. (1891) A case of double consciousness. Proceedings of the Society for Psychical Research 7, 221-58.

Hofstadter, D.R. (1979) Code!, Escher, Bach: An Eternal Golden Braid. London, Penguin.

Hofstadter, D.R. and Dennett, D.C. (eds) (1981) The Mind's I: Fantasies and Reflections on Self and Soul. London, Penguin.

Holland, J. (ed.) (2001) Ecstasy: The Complete Guide: A Comprehensive Look at the Risks and Benefits of MDMA. Rochester, VT, Park Street Press.

Holmes, D.S. (1987) The influence of meditation versus rest on physiological arousal. In M. West (ed.) The Psychology of Meditation. Oxford, Clarendon Press, 81-103.

Holt, J. (1999) Blindsight in debates about qualia. Journal of Consciousness Studies 6(5), 54-71.

Horgan, J. (1994), 'Can science explain consciousness?', Scientific American, 271.

Holloway RL (1996) Evolution of the human brain. In: Lock A, Peters CR (eds) Handbook of human symbolic evolution. Oxford University Press, Oxford

Iacoboni M, Woods RP, Brass M, Bekkering H, Mazziotta JC, Rizzolatti

G (1999) Cortical mechanisms of human imitation. Science 286: 2526–2528.

Iacoboni M, Koski LM, Brass M, Bekkering H, Woods RP, Dubeau MC, Mazziotta JC, Rizzolatti G (2001) Reafferent copies of imitated actions in the right superior temporal cortex. Proc Natl Acad Sci USA 98: 13995–13999.

Jeannerod M (1988) The neural and behavioural organization of goal-directed movements. Clarendon Press, Oxford.

Johnson-Frey SH, Maloof FR, Newman-Norlund R, Farrer C, Inati S, Grafton ST (2003) Actions or hand-objects interactions? Human inferior frontal cortex and action observation. Neuron 39: 1053–1058.

Jackson, F. (1982) Epiphenomenal qualia. Philosophical Quarterly 32, 127-36.

James, W. (1890) The Principles of Psychology (2 volumes). London, Macmillan.

James, W. (1902) The Varieties of Religious Experience: A Study in Human Nature. New York and London, Longmans, Green and Co.

Jansen, K. (2001) Ketamine: Dreams and Realities. Sarasota, FL, Multidisciplinary Association for Psychedelic Studies.

Jay, M. (ed.) (1999) Artificial Paradises: A Drugs Reader. London, Penguin.

Jaynes, J. (1976) The Origin of Consciousness in the Breakdown of the Bicameral Mind. New York, Houghton Mifflin.

Johnson, M.K. and Raye, C.L. (1981) Reality monitoring. Psychological Review 88, 67-85.

Kadim I, Mahgoub O, Baqir S et al. (2015) Cultured meat from muscle stem cells: a review of challenges and prospects. J Integr Agr 14: 222–233

Koski L, Iacoboni M, Dubeau MC, Woods RP, Mazziotta JC (2003) Modulation of cortical activity during different imitative behaviors. J Neurophysiol 89: 460–471.

Krolak-Salmon P, Henaff MA, Isnard J, Tallon-Baudry C, Guenot M, Vighetto A, Bertrand O, Mauguiere F (2003) An attention modulated response to disgust in human ventral anterior insula. Ann Neurol 53: 446–453.

Kandel, E. R. In Search of Memory: The Emergence of a New Science of Mind, W. W. Norton & Company (2007).

Kandel E. R. Schwartz JH, Jessel TM. Principles of neural sciences. New York; McGraw Hill, 2000.

Kanizsa, G. (1979), Organization In Vision (New York: Praeger).

Kaloupek DG, Scott JR, Khatami V. Assessment of coping strategies associated with syncope in blood donors. J Psychosom Res. 1985;29:207-214.

Kanwisher, N. (2001) Neural events and perceptual awareness. Cognition 79, 89-113; also reprinted inS. Dehaene (ed.) The Cognitive Neuroscience of Consciousness. Cambridge, MA, MIT Press, 89-113.

Kapleau, Roshi P. (1980) The Three Pillars of Zen: Teaching, Practice, and Enlightenment (revised edn). New York, Doubleday.

Karn, K. and Hayhoe, M. (2000) Memory representations guide targeting eye movements in a natural task. Visual Cognition 7, 673-703.

Kasamatsu, A. and Hirai, T. (1966) An electroencephalographic study on the Zen meditation (zazen). Folia

Psychiatrica et Neurologica Japonica 20, 315-36.

Kaiserman-Abramof, I. R., Graybiel, A. M., & Nauta, W. J. (1980). The thalamic projection to cortical area 17 in a congenitally anophthalmic mouse strain. Neuroscience, 5, 41–52.

Kanold, P. O., Kara, P., Reid, R. C., & Shatz, C. J. (2003). Role of subplate neurons in functional maturation of visual cortical columns. Science, 301, 521–525.

Kennedy, H., & Dehay, C. (1988). Functional implications of the anatomical organization of the callosal projections of visual areas V1 and V2 in the macaque monkey. Behav. Brain Res., 29, 225–236.

Kentridge, R.W. and Heywood, C.A. (1999) The status of blindsight. Journal of Consciousness Studies 6(5), 3-11.

Kihlstrom, J.F. (1996) Perception without awareness of what is perceived, learning without awareness of what is learned. In M. Velmans (ed.) The Science of Consciousness. London, Routledge, 23-46.

King Jr. Martin Luther, "The Autobiography Of Martin Luther King, Jr.", 1998

Kollerstrom, N. (1999) The path of Halley's comet, and Newton's late apprehension of the law of gravity. Annals of Science 56, 331-56.

Kosslyn, S.M. (1980) Image and Mind. Cambridge, MA, Harvard University Press.

Kosslyn, S.M. (1988) Aspects of a cognitive neuroscience of mental imagery. Science 240, 1621-6.

Kinsbourne, M. (1995), 'The intralaminar thalamic nucleii', Consciousness and Cognition, 4.

Kjaer, Troels, Camilla Bertelsen, Paola Piccini, David Brooks, Jorgen Alving, and Hans Lou. "Increased Dopamine Tone during Meditation- Induced Change of Consciousness." Cognitive Brain Research 13, no. 2 (April 2002)

Kölmel HW. 1985. Complex visual hallucinations in the hemianopic field. J Neurol Neurosurg Psychiatry.

Koenig, Harold. "Research on Religion, Spirituality, and Mental Health: A Review." Canadian Journal of Psychiatry 54, no. 5 (May 2009)

Koenig, Harold, ed. Handbook of Religion and Mental Health. San Diego, CA: Academic Press, 1998

Kraepelin E. Psychiatry: A Textbook for Students and Physicians. New York, NY: Science History Publications; 1990.

Lauglin, Charles, John McManus, and Eugene d'Aquili. Brain, Symbol, and Experience. 2nd ed. New York: Columbia University Press, 1992

Lakoff, G. and M. Johnson (1999). Philosophy in the flesh. Basic Books: New York.

LeDoux, J. E. (1996). The emotional brain. New York: Simon & Schuster.

LeDoux, J.E. (1992), 'Emotion and the amygdala', in The Amygdala: Neurobiological Aspects of Emo- tion, Memory and Mental Dysfunction, ed J.P. Aggleton (New York: Wiley-Liss).

Levin, D.T. and Simons, D.J. (1997) Failure to detect changes to attended objects in motion pictures. Psychonomic Bulletin and Review 4, 501-6.

Levine,J. (1983) Materialism and qualia: the explanatory gap. Pacific Philosophical Quarterly 64, 354-61.

Levine,J. (2001) Purple Haze: The Puzzle of Consciousness. New York, Oxford University Press. Levine, S. (1979) A Gradual Awakening. New York, Doubleday.

Levinson, B.W. (1965) States of awareness during general anaesthesia. British Journal of Anaesthesia 37, 544-6.

Lewicki, P., Czyzewska, M. and Hoffman, H. (1987) Unconscious acquisition of complex procedural knowledge. Journal of Experimental Psychology: Learning, Memory and Cognition 13, 523-30.

Lewicki, P., Hill, T. and Bizot, E. (1988) Acquisition of procedural knowledge about a pattern of stimuli that cannot be articulated. Cognitive Psychology 20, 24-37.

Lewicki, P., Hill, T. and Czyzewska, M. (1992) Nonconscious acquisition of information. American Psychologist 47, 796-801.

Manthey S, Schubotz RI, von Cramon DY (2003). Premotor cortex in observing erroneous action: an fMRI study. Brain Res Cogn Brain Res 15: 296–307.

Mesulam MM, Mufson EJ (1982) Insula of the old world monkey. III: Efferent cortical output and comments on function. J Comp Neurol 212: 38–52.

Naskar, Abhijit. "Homo: A Brief History of Consciousness", 2015

Naskar, Abhijit. "What is Mind?", 2016

Naskar, Abhijit. "Love, God & Neurons: Memoir of A Scientist who found himself by getting lost", 2016

Naskar, Abhijit. "Principia Humanitas", 2017

Naskar, Abhijit. "We Are All Black: A Treatise on Racism", 2017

Naskar, Abhijit. "Either Civilized or Phobic: A Treatise on Homosexuality", 2017

Naskar, Abhijit. "I Am The Thread: My Mission", 2017

Naskar, Abhijit. "The Bengal Tigress: A Treatise on Gender Equality", 2017

Naskar, Abhijit. "Morality Absolute", 2017

Naskar, Abhijit. "Build Bridges not Walls: In the name of Americana", 2018

Naskar, Abhijit. "Fabric of Humanity", 2018

Naskar, Abhijit. "Lives To Serve Before I Sleep", 2019

Naskar, Abhijit. "Citizens of Peace: Beyond the Savagery of Sovereignty", 2019

Naskar, Abhijit. "The Constitution of The United Peoples of Earth", 2019

Naskar, Abhijit. "Neurons Giveth, Neurons Taketh Away | Abhijit Naskar | TEDxIIMRanchi", 2019 https://www.youtube.com/watch?v=BNX-Q0ySm80

Naskar, Abhijit. "Mission Reality", 2019

Naskar, Abhijit. "Operation Justice: To Make A Society That Needs No Law", 2019

Naskar, Abhijit. "Every Generation Needs Caretakers: The Gospel of Patriotism", 2020

Naskar, Abhijit. "Revolution Indomable", 2020

Naskar, Abhijit. "Servitude is Sanctitude", 2020

Naskar, Abhijit. "Good Scientist: When Science and Service Combine", 2020

Naskar, Abhijit. "Sleepless for Society", 2020

Naskar, Abhijit. "Martyr Meets World: To Solve The Hard Problem of Inhumanity", 2021

Newberg, Andrew, and Jeremy Iversen. "The Neural Basis of the

Complex Mental Task of Meditation: Neurotransmitter and Neurochemical Considerations." Medical Hypotheses 61, no. 2 (2003).

Newberg, Andrew. "How God Changes Your Brain: An Introduction to Jewish Neurotheology", CCAR Journal: The Reform Jewish Quarterly, Winter 2016.

Newberg, Andrew, and Stephanie Newberg. "A Neuropsychological Perspective on Spiritual Development." In Handbook of Spiritual Development in Childhood and Adolescence, edited by Eugene Roehlkepartain, Pamela King, Linda Wagener, and Peter Benson. London: Sage Publications, Inc., 2005

Newberg, Andrew. "The Neurotheology Link An Intersection Between Spirituality and Health", Alternative and Complimentary Therapies, Vol 21 No 1, February 2015.

Newberg, Andrew, Nancy Wintering, Dharma Khalsa, Hannah Roggenkamp, and Mark Waldman. "Meditation Effects on Cognitive Function and Cerebral Blood Flow in Subjects with Memory Loss: A Preliminary Study." Journal of Alzheimer's Disease 20, no. 2 (2010)

Nash, M. (1995), 'Glimpses of the mind', Time.

Nesse RM. Proximate and evolutionary studies of anxiety, stress and depression: synergy at the interface. Neurosci Biobehav Rev. 1999;23:895-903.

Nicolelis, Miguel. (2011) "Beyond Boundaries: The New Neuroscience of Connecting Brains with Machines--- and How It Will Change Our Lives", Times Books

O'Hara, K. and Scutt, T. (1996) There is no hard problem of consciousness. Journal of Consciousness Studies 3(4),

290-302, reprinted in J. Shear (ed.) (1997) Explaining Consciousness. Cambridge, MA, MIT Press, 69-82.

O'Regan, J.K. (1992) Solving the "real" mysteries of visual perception: the world as an outside memory. Canadian Journal of Psychology 46, 461-88.

O'Regan, J.K. and Noe, A. (2001) A sensorimotor account of vision and visual consciousness. Behavioral and Brain Sciences 24(5), 883-917.

O'Regan, J.K., Rensink, R.A. and Clark,].]. (1999) Change-blindness as a result of "mudsplashes." Nature 398, 34.

Ornstein, R.E. (1977) The Psychology of Consciousness (2nd edn). New York, Harcourt.

Ornstein, R.E. (1986) The Psychology of Consciousness (3rd edn). New York, Pehguin.

Ornstein, R.E. (1992) The Evolution of Consciousness. New York, Touchstone.

Penfield W, Faulk ME (1955) The insula: further observations on its function. Brain 78: 445– 470.

Penrose, R. (1994), Shadows of the Mind (Oxford: Oxford University Press).

Penrose, R. (1989), The Emperor's New Mind: Concerning Computers, Minds and The Laws of Physics (Oxford: Oxford University Press).

Persinger, "'I would kill in God's name' role of sex, weekly church attendance, report of a religious experience and limbic lability" Perceptual and Motor Skills 1997.

Persinger "Experimental simulation of the God experience" Neurotheology 2003.

Persinger, M. A. (1993b). Personality changes following brain injury as a grief response to the loss of sense of self: Phenomenological themes as indices of local lability and neurocognitive restructuring as psycho- therapy. Psychological Reports, 72

Persinger, Corradini, Clement, Keaney, et al "Neurotheology and its convergence with neuroquantology" NeuroQuantology 2010.

Persinger, Koren and St-Pierre "The electromagnetic induction of mystical and altered states within the laboratory" Journal of Consciousness Exploration and Research 2010.

Persinger "Case report: A prototypical spontaneous 'sensed presence' of a sentient being and concomitant electroencephalographic activity in the clinical laboratory" Neurocase 2008.

Persinger and Saroka "Potential production of Hughlings Jackson's "parasitic consciousness" by physiologically-patterned weak transcerebral magnetic fields: QEEG and source localization" Epilepsy & Behavior 28 (2013).

Persinger. "The neuropsychiatry of paranormal experiences". J Neuropsychiatry Clin Neurosci 2001.

Persinger. "Neuropsychological bases of god beliefs", New York: Praeger, 1987

Persinger. "Temporal lobe epileptic signs and correlative behaviors displayed by normal populations", Journal of General Psychology, 1986

Perry BD, Pollard R. Homeostasis, stress, trauma, and adaptation. A neurodevelopmental view of childhood trauma. Child Adolesc Psychiatr Clin N Am. 1998;7:33.

Paré, D. & Llinás, R. (1995), 'Conscious and preconscious processes as seen from the standpoint of sleep-waking cycle neurophysiology', Neuropsychologia, 33.

P. S. de Laplace. Essai Philosophique sur les Probabilites [1814], in Academy des Sciences, Oeuvres Complotes de Laplace, Vol. 7, Gauthier-Villars, Paris (1886).

Perrett DI, Harries MH, Bevan R, Thomas S, Benson PJ, Mistlin AJ, Chitty AJ, Hietanen JK, Ortega JE (1989) Frameworks of analysis for the neural representation of animate objects and actions. J Exp Bio 146: 87–113.

Phillips ML, Young AW, Senior C, Brammer M, Andrew C, Calder AJ, Bullmore ET, Perrett DI, Rowland D, Williams SC, Gray JA, David AS (1997) A specific neural substrate for perceiving facial expressions of disgust. Nature 389: 495–498.

Phillips ML, Young AW, Scott SK, Calder AJ, Andrew C, Giampietro V, Williams SC, Bullmore ET, Brammer M, Gray JA (1998) Neural responses to facial and vocal expressions of fear and disgust. Proc R Soc Lond B Biol Sci 265: 1809–1817.

Puce A, Perrett D (2003) Electrophysiological and brain imaging of biological motion. Philosoph Trans Royal Soc Lond, Series B, 358: 435–445.

Ramachandran VS. Behavioral and magnetoencephalographic correlates of plasticity in the adult human brain. Proc Natl Acad Sci USA 1993; 90: 10413–20.

Ramachandran VS. Phantom limbs, neglect syndromes, repressed memories, and Freudian psychology. Int Rev Neurobiol 1994; 37: 291–333.

Ramachandran VS. Plasticity and functional recovery in neurology. Clin Med 2005; 5: 368–73.

Ramachandran VS, Hirstein W. The perception of phantom limbs. The D. O. Hebb lecture. Brain 1998; 121: 1603–30.

Ramachandran VS, Rogers-Ramachandran D, Cobb S. Touching the phantom limb. Nature 1995; 377: 489–90.

Ramachandran VS, Rogers-Ramachandran D. Phantom limbs and neural plasticity. Arch Neurol 2000; 57: 317–20.

Ramachandran VS, Rogers-Ramachandran D. It's all done with mirrors. Sci Am Mind 2007; 18: 16–9.

Ramachandran VS, Rogers-Ramachandran D. Sensations referred to a patient's phantom arm from another subjects intact arm: perceptual correlates of mirror neurons. Med Hypotheses 2008; 70: 1233–4.

Ramachandran VS, Rogers-Ramachandran D, Stewart M. Perceptual correlates of massive cortical reorganization. Science 1992; 258: 1159–60.

Rizzolatti G, Craighero L (2004) The mirror-neuron system. Annu Rev Neurosci 27: 169–192.

Rizzolatti G, Fogassi L, Gallese V (2001) Neurophysiological mechanisms underlying the understanding and imitation of action. Nature Rev Neurosci 2:661–670.

Rock I, Victor J. Vision and touch: an experimentally created conflict between the two senses. Science 1964; 143: 594–6.

Rose'n B, Lundborg G. Training with a mirror in rehabilitation of the hand. Scand J Plast Reconstr Surg Hand Surg 2005; 39: 104–8.

Royet JP, Plailly J, Delon-Martin C, Kareken DA, Segebarth C (2003) fMRI of emotional responses to odors: influence of hedonic valence and judgment, handedness, and gender. Neuroimage 20: 713–728.

Rozin R Haidt J and McCauley CR (2000) Disgust. In: Lewis M, Haviland-Jones JM (eds) Handbook of Emotion. 2nd Edition. Guilford Press, New York, pp 637–653.

Saxe R, Carey S, Kanwisher N (2004) Understanding other minds: linking developmental psychology and functional neuroimaging. Annu Rev Psychol 55: 87–124.

S. J. Russell and P. Norvig, Artificial intelligence: a modern approach (3rd edition): Prentice Hall, 2009.

Schienle A, Stark R, Walter B, Blecker C, Ott U, Kirsch P, Sammer G, Vaitl D (2002) The insula is not specifically involved in disgust processing: an fMRI study. Neuroreport 13: 2023–2026.

Showers MJC, Lauer EW (1961) Somatovisceral motor patterns in the insula. J Comp Neurol 117: 107–115.

Singer T, Seymour B, O'Doherty J, Kaube H, Dolan RJ, Frith CD (2004) Empathy for pain involves the affective but not the sensory components of pain. Science 303: 1157–1162.

Smith A (1759) The theory of moral sentiments (ed. 1976). Clarendon Press, Oxford.

S. N. Bose (1924). "Plancks Gesetz und Lichtquantenhypothese". Zeitschrift für Physik. 26 (1): 178–181.

Sprengelmeyer R, Rausch M, Eysel UT, Przuntek H (1998) Neural structures associated with recognition of facial expressions of basic emotions Proc R Soc Lond B Biol Sci 265: 1927–1931.

Strafella AP, Paus T (2000) Modulation of cortical excitability during action observation: a transcranial magnetic stimulation study. NeuroReport 11: 2289–2292.

Simonsen R (2015) Eating for the future: veganism and the challenge of in vitro meat. In: Stapleton P, Byers A (Hg). Biopolitics and utopia. Palgrave Macmillan, New York (2015), S 167–190

Tanaka K (1996) Inferotemporal cortex and object vision. Ann Rev Neurosci. 19: 109–140.

Tesla N. "My Inventions", 1919

T. R. Society, "Machine learning: the power and promise of computers that learn by example," ed. The Royal Society, 2017.

Tomasello M, Call J (1997) Primate cognition. Oxford University Press, Oxford.

Tremblay C, Robert M, Pascual-Leone A, Lepore F, Nguyen DK, Carmant L, Bouthillier A, Theoret H (2004) Action observation and execution: intracranial recordings in a human subject. Neurology. 63: 937–938.

Umilta MA, Kohler E, Gallese V, Fogassi L, Fadiga L, Keysers C, Rizzolatti G (2001) "I know what you are doing": a neurophysiological study. Neuron 32: 91–101.

Von Wright G.H., (1963), Norm and Action. A Logical Inquiry, Routledge & Kegan Paul, London.

Von Wright G.H., (1976), "Determinism and the Study of Man", in Essays on Explanation and Understanding, ed. by J. Manninen and R. Tuomela, Reidel, Dordrecht.

Von Wright G.H., (1977), "What is Humanism?", The Lindlay Lecture, University of Arkansas, Lawrence, Kansas.

Von Wright G.H., (1979), "Humanism and the Humanities", in Philosophy and Grammar, ed. by S. Kanger and S. Öhman, Reidel, Dordrecht, pp. 1-16. Reprinted in von Wright (1993).

Von Wright G.H., (1980), Freedom and Determination, North-Holland Publishing Co., Amsterdam.

Von Wright G.H., (1985), Of Human Freedom, The Tanner Lectures on Human Values,

Vol. VI, ed. by S. M. McMurrin, University of Utah Press, Salt Lake City, pp. 107-70. Reprinted in von Wright (1998).

Von Wright G.H., (1993), The Tree of Knowledge and Other Essays, Brill, Leiden.

Von Wright G.H., (1997), "Progress: Fact and Fiction", in The Idea of Progress, ed. by A. Burgen et al., W. de Gruyter, Berlin, pp. 1-18.

Von Wright G.H., (1998), In the Shadow of Descartes: Essays in the Philosophy of Mind, Kluwer, Dordrecht.